The
VIBRANT
Church

D1365909

About Stan Toler

Dr. Stan Toler has served as a general superintendent in the Church of the Nazarene as well as a pastor for over 40 years in Ohio, Florida, Tennessee, and Oklahoma. He was elected general superintendent emeritus at the 2013 General Assembly in Indianapolis, Indiana. Most recently, Toler was named Founding Executive Director of the Southern Nazarene University Resource Center for Pastoral Leadership.

Stan Toler has written over 100 books, including his best-sellers, *God Has Never Failed Me, But He's Sure Scared Me to Death a Few Times; The Buzzards Are Circling, But God's Not Finished With Me Yet; God's Never Late, He's Seldom Early, He's Always Right on Time; The Secret Blend; The Relational Leader; Practical Guide to Pastoral Ministry; The Inspirational Speaker's Resource, ReThink Your Life*, his popular *Minute Motivator* series, *If Only I Could Relate To The People I'm Related To and his newest book, God Can Do Anything But Fail: So Try Parasailing In A Windstorm*. His books have sold over 3 million copies.

Toler for many years served as Vice-President and taught seminars for John C. Maxwell's INJOY Leadership Institute training church and corporate leaders to make a difference in the world.

He and his wife, Linda, an educator, have two married sons, Seth (Marcy) and Adam (Amanda), and five grandchildren Rhett, Davis, Wren Olivia, Clara Jane, and Bennett.

www.StanToler.com
Follow Stan on Facebook and Twitter

Unless otherwise stated, all Scripture taken from the HOLY BIBLE, NEW INTERNATIONAL VERSION®. Copyright © 1973, 1978, 1984 International Bible Society. Used by permission of Zondervan. All rights reserved.

Contents

A Vibrant Church Is . . .

- a church with an inspiring vision.
- a church with exciting goals.
- a church with practical, proven strategies.
- a church with a pastor who leads.
- a church that is developing committed stewards.
- a church that has meaningful worship.
- a church where every member is a minister.
- a church that effectively cares for the needs of people.
- a church with a plan that will work.

Vibrant Church
YEARLY PLANNER

January
1	
2	
3	
4	

February
1	
2	
3	
4	

March
1	
2	
3	
4	

April
1	
2	
3	
4	

May
1	
2	
3	
4	

June
1	
2	
3	
4	

July
1	
2	
3	
4	

August
1	
2	
3	
4	

September
1	
2	
3	
4	

October
1	
2	
3	
4	

November
1	
2	
3	
4	

December
1	
2	
3	
4	

1. Selections
Vision Sunday
Friendship
Worship
Discipleship
Stewardship
Partnership

2. Sermon Plan
God's Stewards
Words from the Cross
You Asked It
Getting a Glimpse of God
What Jesus Taught
Advent Awakenings

3. Events with a Purpose
Christian Comedy Night
Sweetheart Banquet
Mother's Day
Father's Day
Friend Day
Pastor's Brunch

4. Celebrations
Baptisms
Baby Dedications
Teacher Appreciation
Five-Star Awards
Graduation
Communion

The Vibrant Church

Leading with Vision

Disneyland will never be completed. It will continue to grow as long as there is imagination left in the world.
—Walt Disney

The Vibrant Church

Peter replied, "Repent and be baptized, every one of you, in the name of Jesus Christ for the forgiveness of your sins. And you will receive the gift of the Holy Spirit. The promise is for you and your children and for all who are far off—for all whom the Lord our God will call."

With many other words he warned them; and he pleaded with them, "Save yourselves from this corrupt generation." Those who accepted his message were baptized, and about three thousand were added to their number that day.

They devoted themselves to the apostles' teaching and to the fellowship, to the breaking of bread and to prayer. Everyone was filled with awe, and many wonders and miraculous signs were done by the apostles. All the believers were together and had everything in common. Selling their possessions and goods, they gave to anyone as he had need. Every day they continued to meet together in the temple courts. They broke bread in their homes and ate together with glad and sincere hearts, praising God and enjoying the favor of all the people. And the Lord added to their number daily those who were being saved (Acts 2:38:47).

A Definition of VIBRANT:

The word *VIBRANT* means "resounding life."

Distinguishing Qualities of The VIBRANT Church:

To the weak I became weak, to win the weak. I have become all things to all men so that by all possible means I might save some (I Corinthians 9:22).

1. They have _____ focus.

2. They are _____ and flexible.

3. They are more interested in _____ than copying.

4. They build _____ organizational systems.

5. They are in touch with the surrounding _____.

6. They know how to disagree without being _____.

7. They focus on the human _____ and spiritual hopes.

Immediate Steps to Vibrancy

STEP ONE: BECOME PRAYERFULLY DIAGNOSTIC.

"But you will receive power when the Holy Spirit comes on you; and you will be my witnesses in Jerusalem, and in all Judea and Samaria, and to the ends of the earth" (Acts 1:8).

Vibrancy Questions That Must Be Answered

Session #1   WHERE ARE WE NOW?

What are, and have been, the strengths of our church?

What are, and have been, the limitations of our church?

What needs are being met effectively by our church?

What needs are not being met effectively by our church?

How do we rate?

What drives our church?

What are we doing here?

Why do we exist?

Session #2   WHERE SHALL WE GO?

What is our shared vision for the future of our church?

What general type and style will characterize our church?

What will be the response of our church to the Great Commission?

What if we could start from scratch to build our church?

What is our church doing in regard to the five Ships of Ministry?

What will our church be like in the future?

Session #3 HOW SHALL WE GET THERE?

Who are the people God is calling our church to reach and serve?

What has God called our church to be?

What has God called our church to do?

Who will be the next 100 persons to become members of our church?

Why will they choose our church?

What should be the consequences of our church discovering the role God is calling us to fulfill?

STEP TWO: OVERCOME OBSTACLES.

In the church at Antioch there were prophets and teachers: Barnabas, Simeon called Niger, Lucius of Cyrene, Manaen (who had been brought up with Herod the tetrarch) and Saul. While they were worshiping the Lord and fasting, the Holy Spirit said, "Set apart for me Barnabas and Saul for the work to which I have called them" (Acts 13:1-2).

Growth Inhibitors for the Vibrant Church

1. Leadership models.

2. Grandma syndrome.

3. Fellowship groups.

4. Pastoral staff.

5. Church facilities.

6. Church finances.

7. Ministry misplacement.

8. Pastoral change.

9. Size of community.

10. Pastoral expectations.

STEP THREE: FOCUS ON WHAT GOD WANTS YOU TO DO

Where there is no revelation, the people cast off restraint; but blessed is he who keeps the law (Proverbs 29:18).

1. Develop a mission statement:

Mission
To make Christlike disciples in the nations.

2. Design a corporate vision statement:

Vision

Reaching our friends with the message of salvation. (Friendship)

Expanding ministry involvement at our church. (Partnership)

Activating a deeper commitment to Christ. (Discipleship)

Celebrating hope within our community. (Worship)

Honoring God with our personal resources. (Stewardship)

3. Decide on core values.

Core Values

We value the souls of the lost.	Luke 19:10
We value personal integrity.	Proverbs 10:9
We value corporate worship.	Hebrews 10:25
We value the Word of God.	Deuteronomy 6:6-9
We value the gifts of God's people.	Ephesians 4:11-13
We value wholesome fellowship.	I John 1:7
We value the family of God.	Psalm 133:1

4. Establish strategic priorities.

Recommended Resources: *Pastor's Practical Guide* by Stan Toler

The Vibrant Church

Partnership

Transforming laypersons into leaders will result in an equipped church.

— Stan Toler

Partnership

Launching a Partnership With the Laity

It was he who gave some to be apostles, Some to be prophets, some to be evangelists, and some to be pastors and teachers, to prepare God's people for works of service, so that the body of Christ may be built up until we all reach unity in the faith and in the knowledge of the Son of God and become mature, attaining to the whole measure of the fulness of Christ (Ephesians 4:11-13).

1. Believers are called to minister.
   (1 Peter 2:5,9; 1 Peter 4:10; Ephesians 2:10; 2 Corinthians 5:20)

2. Every believer is gifted by God in unique and specific ways.
   (1 Corinthians 12:4-7; Romans 12:6-8; Ephesians 4:7)

3. One of the most significant roles of the pastor is in equipping the laity for ministry.
   (Ephesians 4:11-13)

4. The church should be both a place for ministry "the church gathered," as well as a base for ministry outside the church "the church scattered."
   (Galatians 6:2,10; Acts 2:42-47; Hebrews 1:24-25)

5. Ministry is serving; it is love in action.
   (John 13:4-5, 14-15; Ephesians 4:12; Matthew 24:35-36, 40; 1 Corinthians 10:31; 1 Corinthians 13)

6. The church will not fully accomplish its mission in the world until laypersons are encouraged to find and fulfill their ministry.
   (1 Corinthians 12:12, 18, 27; Romans 12:4-5; Ephesians 4:11-13; Acts 1:8; Matthew 28:19-20; John 20:21)

Source: Gary Morsch

Why Build a Ministry Team?

1. Shared vision and values. 1 Peter 2:5

2. It's biblical. Romans 12:4-5

3. It's more effective. Ecclesiastes 4:9-10

My Ministry Profile

Purpose _____

Personality _____

Passion _____

Plans _____

S piritual Gifts

H eart for Ministry

A bility – Giftedness

P ersonality

E xperience

—Rick Warren

Launching Ministry Action Teams

1. Select and train a team leader.

2. Form a ministry action team.

3. Create vision and purpose.

4. Establish accountability lines.

5. Develop realistic goals.

6. Empower and release.

7. Affirm and recognize.

8. Streamline the structure.

*Any organization that intends to grow
must be a learning organization.*
—Peter Senge

Recommended Resources: *Leader Coach* by Stan Toler and Larry Gilbert; *Church Operations Manual* by Stan Toler

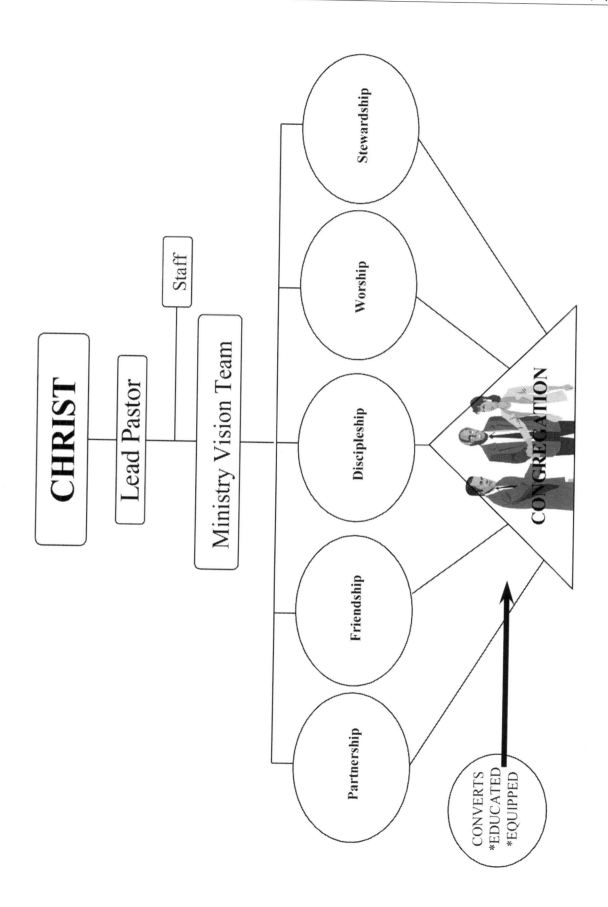

WESLEYAN INVESTMENT FOUNDATION
Serving Higher Interests™

Investment opportunities for both individuals and organizations

- Save money

- Earn interest

- Build churches

- Change lives

Save for the things that are important to you and your family and build the Kingdom at the same time!

Contact us today for more information:
317.774.7300
info@wifonline.com
www.wifonline.com

The Vibrant Church

Friendship

Christians need to stop thinking
evangelism is a spiritual gift.
— Ed Stetzer

Friendship

Passionate Evangelism

Then Jesus came to them and said, "All authority in heaven and on earth has been given to me. Therefore go and make disciples of all nations, baptizing them in the name of the Father and of the Son and of the Holy Spirit, and teaching them to obey everything I have commanded you. And surely I am with you always, to the very end of the age" (Matthew 28:18-20).

1. Evangelism is a process of communication.

2. Evangelism produces spiritual life.

3. Evangelism meets needs.

4. Evangelism is sharing the good news.

5. Evangelism is only effective when a person enters a relationship with Christ.

WITNESS (wit'nes) *n.* 1. a. One who has seen or heard something. b. One who gives evidence. 2. To serve as or furnish evidence of.

Effective Evangelism Methods:

After they prayed, the place where they were meeting was shaken. And they were all filled with the Holy Spirit and spoke the word of God boldly (Acts 4:31).

1. Prayer evangelism.

2. Needs evangelism.

- Preaching
- Divorce Recovery
- Grief Recovery
- Day Care / Schools
- Community Business Day
- 12-Step Recovery Program
- Counseling
- Small Groups / Sunday School
- English as a Second Language
- Financial Freedom

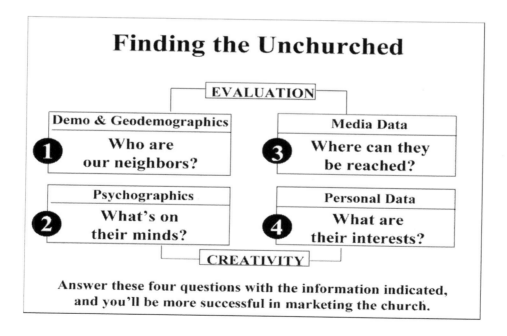

3. Relationship evangelism.

The Circle of Friends

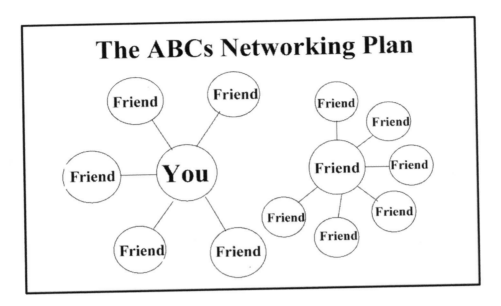

A. Pray for them daily.

B. Share four activities with them during the next year.

Possible Activities

- Sporting Events
- Coffee Shop
- Cook-outs
- Banquets
- Tours
- Drama at your church
- Community Events

- Shopping
- Civic Clubs
- Golf Outings
- Birthdays/Anniversaries
- Desserts at your place
- Breakfasts/Luncheons

C. Invite them to an event for the unchurched.

4. Event evangelism.

- Concert
- Children's Program
- Christmas Musical
- Revival
- Friend Day
- Christian Comedy
- Drama
- Easter Musical
- Guest Artist Series
- Seminars
- Pumpkin Patch

Special Note: Design a response form for each special event.

Example: At the mid-point of your special event presentation, plan to share the *ABC* plan. Be sure to ask <u>everyone</u> to fill out the information form and ask <u>everyone</u> to pray.

THE ABC'S OF A PERSONAL RELATIONSHIP WITH CHRIST

Receiving Jesus Christ is as simple as ABC . . .

A dmit that you have sinned.   Romans 3:23

B elieve that Jesus Christ died for you.   John 1:12

C onfess that Jesus Christ is Lord of your life.   Romans 10:9

"Dear Lord Jesus, I know that I am a sinner. I believe that You died for my sins and arose from the grave. I now turn from my sins and invite You to come into my heart and life. I receive You as my personal Savior and follow You as my Lord. Amen"

Recommended Resource: ABCs of Evangelism by Stan Toler

5. Deeds evangelism.

6. Media evangelism.

- TV
- Radio
- Yellow Pages
- Newspaper
- Direct Mail
- Website

7. Worship evangelism.

8. Church planting evangelism.

87% of Protestant churches are stagnant or declining in the USA.

—Conrad Lowe

Recommended Resources: *ABCs of Evangelism* by Stan Toler; How to Go to Heaven Pens www.abcpens.com

The Vibrant Church

Discipleship

*Our goal should be to make Christlike
disciples in the nations.*
— Jesse C. Middendorf

Intentional Discipleship

The process of evangelizing is not complete until those who have responded to the claims of Christ are active, functioning members of a local church. In other words, the goal in evangelism is not to get "decisions," but to make "disciples."

—Robert Bast

What Is A Disciple?

1. A disciple is a student. Luke 6:40

2. A disciple is a steward. Galatians 5:22-23

3. A disciple is a servant. Romans 1:1

Eight Disciplines of Every Follower of Christ:

1. Pursuing holiness.

Therefore, I urge you, brothers, in view of God's mercy, to offer your bodies as living sacrifices, holy and pleasing to God—this is your spiritual act of worship. 2Do not conform any longer to the pattern of this world, but be transformed by the renewing of your mind. Then you will be able to test and approve what God's will is—his good, pleasing and perfect will (Romans 12:1-2).

2. Private worship.

Let us then approach the throne of grace with confidence, so that we may receive mercy and find grace to help us in our time of need (Hebrews 4:16).

3. Public worship.

Worship the LORD with gladness; come before him with joyful songs (Psalm 100:2).

4. Observing sacraments.

Therefore, whoever eats the bread or drinks the cup of the Lord in an unworthy manner will be guilty of sinning against the body and blood of the Lord. [28]A man ought to examine himself before he eats of the bread and drinks of the cup. [29]For anyone who eats and drinks without recognizing the body of the Lord eats and drinks judgment on himself (1 Corinthians 11:27-29).

5. Personal witnessing.

He told them, "This is what is written: The Christ will suffer and rise from the dead on the third day, and repentance and forgiveness of sins will be preached in his name to all nations, beginning at Jerusalem. You are witnesses of these things. I am going to send you what my Father has promised; but stay in the city until you have been clothed with power from on high" (Luke 24:46-48).

6. Personal discipline.

"But I have prayed for you, Simon, that your faith may not fail. And when you have turned back, strengthen your brothers" (Luke 22:32).

7. Biblical stewardship.

The earth is the Lord's, and everything in it, the world, and all who live in it; (Psalm 24:1)

8. Church membership.

Husbands, love your wives, just as Christ loved the church and gave himself up for her to make her holy, cleansing her by the washing with water through the word, and to present her to himself as a radiant church, without stain or wrinkle or any other blemish, but holy and blameless (Ephesians 5:25-27).

12 Stone Five Step Process

1. Know your culture.

2. Model your culture.

3. Communicate your culture.

4. Correct drift in your culture.

5. Celebrate your culture.

—Pastor Kevin Myers

Recommended Resources: *Ministry Motivators for Believers* by Stan Toler; *Home Run* by Kevin Myers and John C. Maxwell

Pastor's Welcome Class	Gifts Discovery Class	Discipleship Class
Week 1 – Vision	Week 1 – Personality Profiles	Week 1 – Beliefs
Week 2 – Confidence	Week 2 – Interest and Skills	Week 2 – Core Values
Week 3 – Communication	Week 3 – Spiritual Gifts I	Week 3 – Stewardship
Week 4 – Family	Week 4 – Spiritual Gifts II	Week 4 – Lay Ministry
4 Weeks	**4 Weeks**	**4 Weeks**

Recommended Resources: *Growing Christians Kit* by Stan Toler; *Community Minded Church* by Stan Toler; *Year Round Book of Events and Celebrations* by Stan Toler; *Terrific! Five Star Customer Service* by Stan Toler

WESLEYAN INVESTMENT FOUNDATION
Serving Higher Interests™

Providing faith based, loan and savings opportunities since 1946.

- Church Loans

- Regular Savings

- IRA Savings

Contact us today for more information:
317.774.7300
info@wifonline.com
www.wifonline.com

The Vibrant Church

Worship

Worship involves the giving of ourselves. It is a movement of our hearts, our thoughts and our wills.

— Darlene Zschech

Meaningful Worship

A Working Definition: "Worship is the human response to divine revelation. Being a personal worshiper is central to experiencing transformation."

—Terry N. Toler

Every Believer Needs 3 Experiences Each Week

1. Community worship.

2. Community fellowship.

3. Community service.

Worship Hinderances

1. Lack of prayer. Psalm 24:1-10

2. Limited Biblical knowledge. Ephesians 6:17

3. Wrong attitudes. 1 Peter 2:2-3

4. A deceitful heart. Acts 5:4-5

5. A spirit of unforgiveness. 1 John 1:7–9

Insights About Worship

1. We do not need a building to worship.

2. There is no correct style of worship.

3. True worship answers the questions about God and life.

4. Worship is a powerful witness to the unchurched.

Planning for Worship

1. Identify the goal of the service.

2. Identify the message that will be communicated.

3. Identify the target audience that you want to reach.

Ingredients of Passionate Worship

Adoration   Psalm 29:2

Confession   John 4:24

Thanksgiving   Ephesians 5:19

Supplication   Acts 4:31

> *"44% of the people who attend church last year said that they did not experience God in worship."*
> — George Barna

WESLEYAN INVESTMENT FOUNDATION
Serving Higher Interests™

WIF provides loans for churches and church related organizations in the the Wesleyan Tradition.

Capital projects include:

- New Construction
  - Renovation
  - Relocation
  - Refinance

Competitive Rates

Flexible Terms

Low Closing Costs

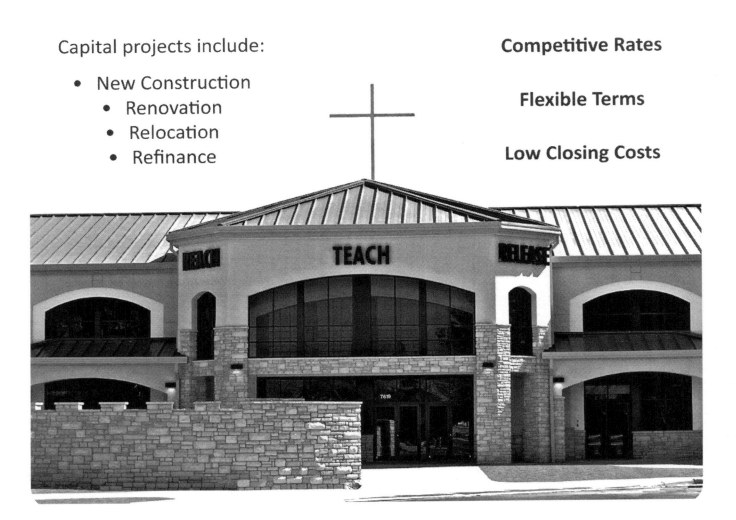

It would be our privilege to be your ministry partner!

Contact us today for more information:
317.774.7300
info@wifonline.com
www.wifonline.com

The Vibrant Church

Stewardship

Giving is the result of an inspired motive.
— Melvin Maxwell

Stewardship

Developing a Culture of Generosity

For I testify that they gave as much as they were able, and even beyond their ability. Entirely on their own, they urgently pleaded with us for the privilege of sharing in this service to the saints. And they did not do as we expected but they gave themselves first to the Lord and then to us in keeping with God's will (2 Corinthians 8:3-5).

Barriers to Donor Generosity

1. History of entitlement.

2. Culture of scarcity.

3. Attitude of materialism.

4. Feelings of doubt.

5. Absence of teaching.

6. Spirit of indifference.

7. Pattern of abuse.

> **People give better when their gifts are appreciated.**
> —Stan Toler

Raising Up Generous Givers

1. Stewardship education.

2. Purposeful motivation.

3. Systematic invitation.

4. Meaningful celebration.

Recommended Resources: *Give to Live* by Stan Toler; *It's Not About The Money* by Terry Munday; *Developing A Giving Church* by Elmer Towns and Stan Toler: *Cycle of Victorious Giving* by Stan and Linda Toler

Media Recommendations: www.kluth.org, stewardshipcentral.com, www.stantoler.com, www.stewardshipkids.com, www.stewardshiptechnologies.com, www.bgwservices.com

The Vibrant Church

Appendix

Planning Process

Vibrant Church Project Ships of Ministry Selections
(Monthly)

1. Partnership

2. Friendship

3. Discipleship

4. Worship

5. Stewardship

Sermon Series
(Identify at least 12 topics)

1. The Christian Calendar/Special Seasons.

2. Messages relating to 5 Ships of Ministry.

3. Felt Needs.

4. Expositions/Preaching through a book of the Bible.

5. Lectionary use (if applicable).

Events With A Purpose
(Plan one unchurched event per quarter.)

Celebrations
(Plan one per month.)

Vibrant Church Preparation Months

Month One Checklist:

❏ Diagnosis/Mission Statement.
❏ Vision Planning/Vision Statement.
❏ Selection of "Ships of Ministry."
❏ Qualities of a Great Church (possible sermon series).

Month Two Checklist:

❏ Goal-Setting.
❏ Strategic Planning of 4 Unchurched Events.
❏ Strategic Planning of 12 Celebrations.

Month Three:
(Sample Only)

❏ Begin Pastor's Welcome Class.
❏ Implement Leadership Training.
❏ Begin Lay Training and Recruitment.
❏ Usher/Greeter Training.

Vision Sunday:

❏ One Year Sermon Plan Begins.
  • Communicate the vision - visually (PowerPoint, Overhead, Videos, etc.)
  • Display banners, distribute vision statement cards, etc.

VIBRANT CHURCH PLANNER

January

1	Stewardship
2	Loving God . . . Loving Each Other
3	Pie Auction
4	Baby Dedication

February

1	Partnership
2	REACH
3	Sweetheart Banquet
4	Baptism

March

1	Partnership
2	Words from the Cross
3	Pastor's Brunch
4	Five-Star Awards

April

1	Worship
2	Making the Most of Your Worship Experience
3	Good Friday Luncheon
4	Seder Feast

May

1	Partnership
2	Special Days (Baby Day, Mother's Day, Memorial Day)
3	Mother's Day
4	Graduation

June

1	Discipleship
2	You Asked It
3	Father's Day
4	Communion

July

1	Friendship
2	You Asked It
3	Pastor's Lunch
4	Baptism

August

1	Partnership
2	You Asked It
3	Upward Soccer
4	Teacher Appreciation/ Commissioning

September

1	Discipleship
2	Getting a Glimpse of God
3	FCA Game Day
4	Children's Ministry Kick-Off

October

1	Friendship
2	What Jesus Taught
3	Pumpkin Patch
4	Pastor Appreciation

November

1	Discipleship
2	What Jesus Taught
3	Revival Sunday
4	Hanging of the Greens

December

1	Worship
2	Advent Awakenings
3	Christmas Concert
4	Candlelight Communion

50 IDEAS INTO YOUR Community

by David Drury

We are seeing God transform lives, churches, and communities with the hope and holiness of Jesus Christ in The Wesleyan Church. What are some practical ways we can offer hope in his name? How is an intentionally missional holiness applied in our hurting local communities?

We've asked pastors and laypeople and received scores of ideas for demonstrating love and hope in Christ. Which of these do you already do and which ones could you start? Let us know what you would add to the list!

SPECIAL SPACES

23 Use church facility as a safe place for at-risk kids after school
24 Religious instruction in public school arrangements
25 Convert the old parsonage into a need-meeting station
26 Organize a kid/parent breakfast at school
27 Let neighborhood use church parking lot for block party
28 Host art show with community and school artists
29 Be generous in making church available for weddings, etc.

EMPOWERING PEOPLE

1 Make and freeze meals alongside those in need
2 Community garden: teach others to plant, harvest, & share
3 Offer ESL (English as a Second Language) classes
4 Teach car maintenance
5 Teach kids to fix bicycles
6 Offer biblical finance classes
7 Teach Spanish or other secondary local languages

BUILDING RELATIONSHIPS

30 Befriend someone trapped in poverty
31 Have a conversation with anyone you give something to
32 Encourage schoolteachers and first-responders
33 Host a meal for veterans
34 Visit shut-ins
35 Food night at church (visitors eat free!)
36 Recruit foster/adoptive parents

GENEROUS LIVING

8 Provide coins at laundromats
9 Give to relief efforts for those in desperate times
10 Keep a guest room occupied
11 Provide transportation
12 Put together holiday meal packages for families in need
13 Give baby care items to pregnant teens and others in need
14 Make it easy for the community to use church facilities
15 Fill backpacks with school supplies for needy kids

MEETING NEEDS

37 Clothing drives
38 Set up a group home or serve there
39 Sponsor newly arriving immigrants
40 Assist Native communities
41 Free medical screening days
42 Open a church facility overnight for the homeless
43 Open or partner at a community food & essentials pantry
44 Assist neighbors/victims after storms

CARING COMPASSION

16 Offer marriage/family counseling
17 Local hotline for key needs
18 Sit with people during chemo or other medical situations
19 Support and traning for mental illness
20 Depression support groups
21 Recovery programs
22 Combat human trafficking

INTENTIONAL PARTNERSHIPS

45 Police and firefighters
46 Salvation Army and rescue missions
47 Community centers
48 Neighborhood associations
49 School administration
50 Health and Human Services

Used with permission

WORKBOOK SPONSORS

WESLEYAN INVESTMENT FOUNDATION
Serving Higher Interests™

Free financial seminars now available!

The goal of these seminars is to highlight the importance of supporting the ministries of the local church as well as the Kingdom and stewardship benefits of investing with WIF.

- Presented during a time that works the best for your church family.

- No cost to the local church.

- WIF provides the refreshments!

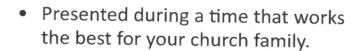

Contact us today for more information:
317.774.7300
info@wifonline.com
www.wifonline.com

BUILD A KIT
BUILD YOUR TEAM
MAKE AN IMPACT.

You can make a difference in the lives of people around the world by hosting a kit assembly event.

Your team will build specialized kits that directly impact the health and well-being of children, women and men in need.

PowrServ events benefit
Heart to Heart International.

Contact:

Bethany Williams
913.538.7892
bethany.williams@powrserv.org

@PowrServ
Facebook.com/PowrServ

Christian Healthcare Ministries
The biblical solution to healthcare costs
www.chministries.org

ACCREDITED CHARITY
bbb.org
BBB

1.800.791.6225
www.facebook.com/christianhealthcareministries
www.chministries.org

35 YEARS

STewardship PAYROLL SERVICES

Working with ministries nationwide!

As little as $2 per person, per payroll period

✓ **Easy to use**
✓ **Totally on-line**
✓ **Secure**
✓ **No year-end or W-2 fees**

CONTACT: Gerry Washington
866-604-8880, ext.706

gerry@stewardshiptechnology.com
www.stewardshippayroll.com

AMERICA'S CHRISTIAN
CREDIT UNION

proud partner of

stewardship technology
serving the church through technology

ELECTRONIC GIVING SOLUTIONS

The secure and economical way to accept donations electronically!

Designed specifically for your church or ministries unique needs. Electronic Giving Solutions by Stewardship Technology provides a safe and secure way to accept tithes, offerings and general donations.

With Electronic Giving Solutions, you can:
· Turn occasional givers into consistent year-round donors
· Improve your ability to predict cash flow
· Access donor data through our online Beneficiary Web
· Easily download accounting reports
· Provide donors with a simple, fast way to manage their giving

IS YOUR CHURCH ONLINE?

GET STARTED TODAY!
Call **Gerry** at **866-604-8880, ext. 706** or go to **www.egsnetwork.com**

Stewardship Technology, Inc. Mount Vernon, OH 43050 | www.StewardshipTechnology.com

stewardship technology
serving the church through technology

TOLER LEADERSHIP

Call 405.603.7110 | Fax 405.603.7120 | Email info@tolerleadership.com
Mail: PO Box 720230 – Oklahoma City OK 73172

Humor/Inspiration	QTY	RETAIL PRICE	SALE PRICE	TOTAL PRICE
Buzzards Are Circling But God's Not Finished With Me Yet		$15.00	$10.00	
God Has Never Failed Me, But He's Sure Scared Me To Death A Few Times		$15.00	$10.00	
God Can Do Anything But Fail, So Try Parasailing In A Windstorm - NEW		$15.00	$10.00	
ReThink Your Life		$22.00	$10.00	
ReThink Your Life Journal		$10.00	$5.00	
That Ain't Just Preaching		$13.00	$5.00	
You Might Be a Preacher If (BEST OF)		$7.00	$5.00	
You've Been Around the Church a Long Time		$7.00	$5.00	
Minute Motivator Series				
Minute Motivators for Dieters		$7.00	$5.00	
Minute Motivators for Graduates		$7.00	$5.00	
Minute Motivators For Leaders		$7.00	$5.00	
Minute Motivators for Men		$7.00	$5.00	
Minute Motivators for the Military - NEW		$7.00	$5.00	
Minute Motivators for New Believers - NEW		$7.00	$5.00	
Minute Motivators for Teachers		$7.00	$5.00	
Minute Motivators for Teens		$7.00	$5.00	
Minute Motivators for Women		$7.00	$5.00	
Minute Motivators for Athletes		$7.00	$5.00	
Leadership				
The Exceptional Leader		$16.00	$10.00	
The Relational Leader		$18.00	$10.00	
The Secret Blend		$18.00	$10.00	
Outstanding! Leadership that Motivates and Relates - NEW		$14.00	$10.00	
Terrific! Five Star Customer Service - NEW		$11.00	$10.00	
Total Quality Life		$15.00	$10.00	
How to Capture Your Thought Life		$8.00	$5.00	
How to Shape Up Your Health		$8.00	$5.00	
How to Gain Control of Your Finances		$8.00	$5.00	
How to Strengthen Your Faith		$8.00	$5.00	
Pastoral Resources				
The Case of Stuart's Ship (Children's Book)		$15.00	$10.00	
Each One Win One		$30.00	$10.00	
Each One Disciple One		$30.00	$10.00	
Give to Live		$17.00	$10.00	
ReThink Your Life		$20.00	$10.00	
Stan Toler's Practical Guide for Pastoral Ministry		$18.00	$10.00	
Stan Toler's Practical Guide for Hiring Staff		$15.00	$5.00	
Stan Toler's Practical Guide for Ministry Transition		$15.00	$5.00	
Stan Toler's Practical Guide for Leading Church Boards		$15.00	$5.00	
Stan Toler's Practical Guide for Leading Staff		$15.00	$5.00	
Stan Toler's Practical Guide for Solo Ministry		$15.00	$5.00	
Devotions for Ministry Couples		$15.00	$5.00	
Devotions for Pastors		$15.00	$5.00	
The Five Star Church		$17.00	$10.00	
The Vibrant Church		$13.00	$5.00	
You Might Be a Preacher If (BEST OF)		$7.00	$5.00	
You've Been Around the Church a Long Time		$7.00	$5.00	
He Still Speaks – Toler Brothers CD		$20.00	$5.00	
			TOTAL	

Ordering Options

PO Box 720230 – Oklahoma City, OK 73172 | Phone 405-603-7110 (CREDIT CARD)| Fax 405-603-7120

Books for Annual Special Events

JANUARY – Stewardship Emphasis
- ☐ *Give to Live - $17.99*
- ☐ *How to Gain Control of Your Finances - $7.99*
- ☐ *ReThink Your Life - 22.99*
- ☐ *ReThink Journal - $9.99*
- ☐ *Minute Motivators for Dieters - $6.99*

FEBRUARY – Valentines Day Emphasis
- ☐ *Devotions for Ministry Couples - $12.99*

MARCH – Outreach and Evangelism Emphasis
- ☐ *The Secret Blend - $17.99*
- ☐ *Minute Motivators for New Believers - $6.99*
- ☐ *Each One Win One - $29.99*
- ☐ *Each One Disciple One - $29.99*

APRIL – Memorial Day Emphasis
- ☐ *Minute Motivators for the Military - $6.99*

MAY – Mother's Day Emphasis
- ☐ *Minute Motivators for Women - $6.99*
- ☐ *Buzzards Are Circling; But God's Not Finished With Me Yet - $14.99*
- ☐ *God's Never Failed Me; But He's Sure Scared Me To Death A Few Times - $14.99*

JUNE – Dad and Grad's Day Emphasis
- ☐ *Minute Motivators for Graduates - $6.99*
- ☐ *The Winning Dad - $12.99*
- ☐ *Minute Motivators for Men - $6.99*
- ☐ *Minute Motivators for Athletes - $6.99*

JULY – Leadership/Church Boards
- ☐ *The Exceptional Leader - $15.99*

- ☐ *Minute Motivators for Leaders - $6.99*
- ☐ *Practical Guide for Church Boards - $14.99*
- ☐ *Practical Guide for Hiring Staff - $14.99*
- ☐ *Practical Guide for Hiring Staff - $14.99*
- ☐ *Practical Guide for Solo Ministry - $14.99*
- ☐ *Practical Guide for Ministry Transition - $14.99*

AUGUST – Youth/Teacher Emphasis
- ☐ *Minute Motivators for Teens - $6.99*
- ☐ *Minute Motivators for Teachers - $6.99*

SEPTEMBER – Outreach and Evangelism
- ☐ *The Relational Leader - $17.99*
- ☐ *Minute Motivators for New Believers - $6.99*
- ☐ *Total Quality Life - $14.99*

OCTOBER – Pastor Appreciation
- ☐ *Devotions for Pastors*
- ☐ *The Best of You Might Be A Preacher if... - $6.99*
- ☐ *That Ain't Just Preaching; A View From the Back Pew - $13.00*
- ☐ *You've Know You've Been Around Church Too Long.... - $6.99*
- ☐ *Pastor's Practical Guide For Ministry - $17.99*

NOVEMBER – Veteran's Day
- ☐ *Minute Motivators for the Military - $6.99*

DECEMBER – Year End Giving/Donor Gifts
- ☐ *How to Strengthen Your Faith - $7.99*
- ☐ *How to Shape Up Your Health - $7.99*
- ☐ *How to Capture Your Thought Life - $7.99*
- ☐ *How To Gain Control of Your Finances - $7.99*

Pricing Breakdown

Books that **retail for $10.00 or more are $5.00 each** in quantities of 25 or more. (Plus Shipping)

Books that **retail for less than $10.00 are $3.00 each** in quantities of 25 or more. (Plus Shipping)

For descriptions and images of each book please visit **www.StanToler.com**

Ordering Options

PO Box 720230 – Oklahoma City, OK 73172 | Phone 405-603-7110 | Fax 405-603-7120

The Vibrant Church

This is to certify that

has completed *The Vibrant Church* training conference involving four hours of instruction, to be transferred into the amount of continuing education credits as determined by the certificate holder's crediting organization.

Awarded _____ (Date), in _____ (City/ State)

Stan Toler, Instructor

"...when the wise are instructed, they receive knowledge"
Proverbs 21:11.

47718435R00030

Made in the USA
San Bernardino, CA
06 April 2017